W9-AYX-858

# SIMPLE MACHINES
# Screws

by Kay Manolis

BLASTOFF! 4 READERS

BELLWETHER MEDIA • MINNEAPOLIS, MN

Note to Librarians, Teachers, and Parents:

**Blastoff! Readers** are carefully developed by literacy experts and combine standards-based content with developmentally appropriate text.

**Level 1** provides the most support through repetition of high-frequency words, light text, predictable sentence patterns, and strong visual support.

**Level 2** offers early readers a bit more challenge through varied simple sentences, increased text load, and less repetition of high-frequency words.

**Level 3** advances early-fluent readers toward fluency through increased text and concept load, less reliance on visuals, longer sentences, and more literary language.

**Level 4** builds reading stamina by providing more text per page, increased use of punctuation, greater variation in sentence patterns, and increasingly challenging vocabulary.

**Level 5** encourages children to move from "learning to read" to "reading to learn" by providing even more text, varied writing styles, and less familiar topics.

Whichever book is right for your reader, Blastoff! Readers are the perfect books to build confidence and encourage a love of reading that will last a lifetime!

This edition first published in 2010 by Bellwether Media, Inc.

No part of this publication may be reproduced in whole or in part without written permission of the publisher. For information regarding permission, write to Bellwether Media, Inc., Attention: Permissions Department, Post Office Box 19349, Minneapolis, MN 55419.

Library of Congress Cataloging-in-Publication Data
Manolis, Kay.
   Screws / by Kay Manolis.
     p. cm. — (Blastoff! readers. Simple machines)
Includes bibliographical references and index.
   Summary: "Simple text, full color photographs, and illustrations introduce beginning readers to the basic principles of screws. Developed by literary experts for students in grades 2 through 5"—Provided by publisher.
   ISBN 978-1-60014-322-9 (hardcover : alk. paper)
   1. Screws—Juvenile literature. I. Title.

TJ1338.M32 2010
621.8'82—dc22                                      2009008272

# Contents

# What Is a Screw?

Have you ever tried to take the lid off a jar? The lid is a **screw**. A screw is a **simple machine**. A simple machine has few or no moving parts. Simple machines make **work** easier. You do work when you move objects from one place to another.

You use **force** when you do work. Force causes objects to start moving, stop moving, or change direction. You use force when you climb the monkey bars at a playground. The amount of force you use is called **effort**. Simple machines reduce the amount of effort needed to do a job.

# How Screws Work

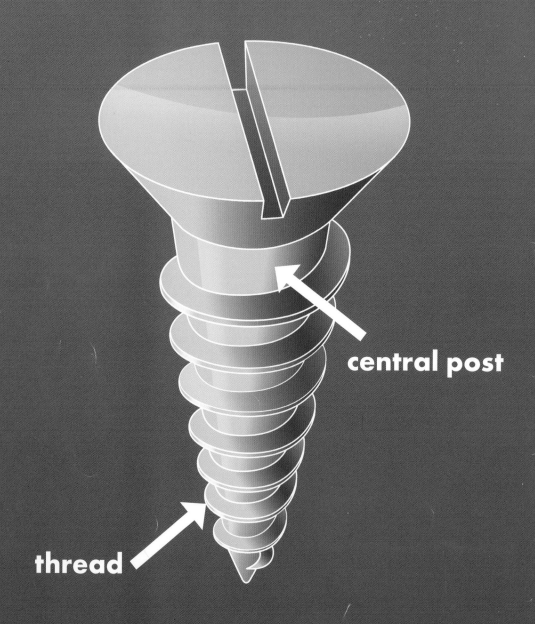

central post

thread

A screw has two parts. They are the central post and the ridge wrapped around it. The ridge is called the **thread**. It has a spiral shape. The thread acts like a **ramp**. A ramp is another simple machine that is used to move objects from one level to another.

**fun fact**

Over 2,000 years ago, a man named Archimedes invented a machine with a screw to collect water.

The distance between each turn of the thread on a screw is called the **pitch**. A screw moves the same distance as the pitch with each full turn. You use less effort to turn a screw with a low pitch. Each turn only moves the screw a short distance. You use more effort to turn a screw with a high pitch. Each turn moves the screw a longer distance.

high pitch ◀

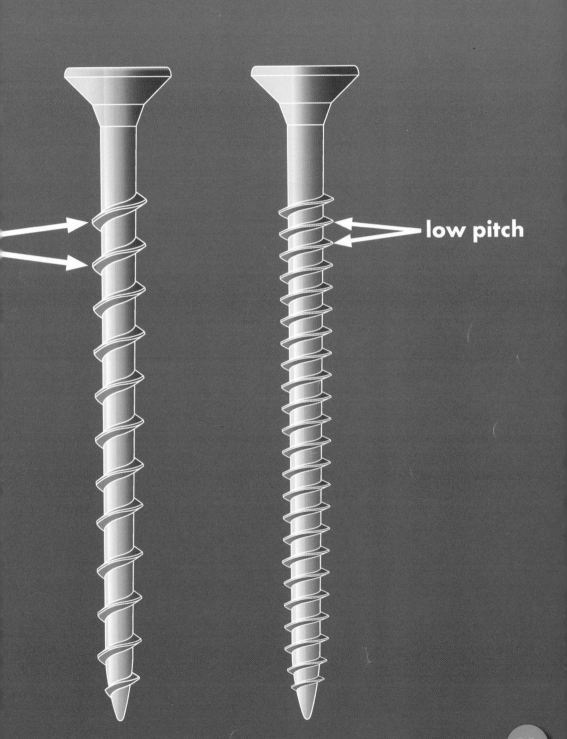

**low pitch**

11

# Examples of Screws

There are many different types of screws. Some fasten objects together. Carpenters use thousands of screws to build houses. Walls, windows, and doors are held in place by screws.

**!** **fun fact**

Large screws were used in the 1600s to make coins. A screw with a design on one end was pressed into a piece of metal. This piece of metal became a coin.

Other screws flatten things. This is called **pressing**. Machines with large screws grind vegetables and nuts to make oil.

Some screws lift and lower objects as they turn. Snowblowers use large screws called **augers** to lift snow off the ground and blow it away.

Small augers are used to drill holes into wood. An auger lifts wood shavings out of a hole with each turn. Some augers are used in cleaning jobs. Plumbers use long augers to clean pipes.

Boats and airplanes use rotating screws called **propellers** to help them move through water and air.

Propellers have two or more curved blades that spin in a circle. When the spinning blades push against water or air, the boats and airplanes move forward or backward.

threads

You can find many other examples of screws around you. Do you turn on a light when it gets dark? A light bulb is a screw. The screw's thread is at the base of the bulb.

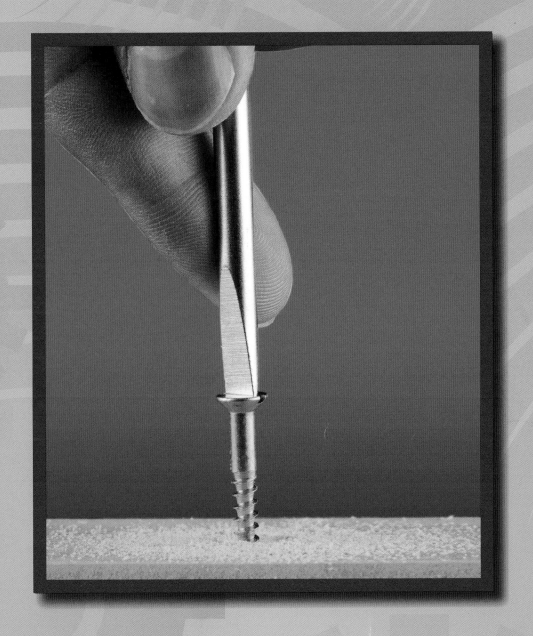

The furniture in your house is held together with many screws. Carpenters use them to build tables, chairs, and beds.

# Screws and Complex Machines

Screws are often parts of **complex machines**. A complex machine is made of two or more simple machines that work together. Complex machines have many moving parts. A bicycle is a complex machine. The wheels, seat, and handlebars attach to the bicycle frame with screws. It would be difficult to ride a bicycle without screws!

# Glossary

**auger**—a type of screw that lifts and lowers objects with each turn

**complex machine**—a machine made of two or more simple machines that work together

**effort**—the amount of force needed to move an object from one place to another

**force**—a push or pull that causes an object to move, change its direction, or stop moving

**pitch**—the distance between each turn of a thread on a screw

**pressing**—to flatten something with a machine

**propeller**—a rotating screw with curved blades that pushes against air or water

**ramp**—a simple machine used to move loads from one level to another

**screw**—a simple machine that fastens materials together, lifts and lowers materials, or presses objects flat

**simple machine**—a machine that has few or no moving parts

**thread**—the ridge that wraps in a spiral shape around the central post of a screw

**work**—to move an object from one place to another

# To Learn More

**AT THE LIBRARY**
Douglas, Lloyd G. *What Is a Screw?* New York, N.Y.: Children's Press, 2002.

Gardner, Robert. *Sensational Science Projects with Simple Machines.* Berkley Heights, N.J.: Enslow, 2006.

Glover, David. *Screws.* Chicago, Ill.: Heinemann, 2006.

**ON THE WEB**
Learning more about simple machines is as easy as 1, 2, 3.

1. Go to www.factsurfer.com.

2. Enter "simple machines" into the search box.

3. Click the "Surf" button and you will see a list of related Web sites.

With factsurfer.com, finding more information is just a click away.

# Index

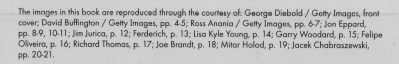